LET'S MAKE A DIFFERENCE:

Learning About
OUR OCEAN

Gabriella Francine
with Solara Vayanian

Illustrations by Phil Velikan

BBM BOOKS

Layout, cover and illustrations by Phil Velikan www.findphil.com
Editorial assistance provided by Dorothy Chambers
Packaged by Wish Publishing
Special thanks to Mahmood Rezai for his support of this title and Big Blue Marble.

Printed in the United States of America
10 9 8 7 6 5 4 3 2 1

Published by BBM Books

Photography credits

Cover photo: © Vilainecrevette/Shutterstock
Title page: © njaj/Shutterstock
Dedication page: © Rich Carey/Shutterstock
Pages 2-3: © Vilainecrevette/Shutterstock
Page 3: Plankton© bluehand/Shutterstock
Page 4: © worldswildlifewonders/Shutterstock
Page 5: © kozer/Shutterstock
Page 6: Beach © Mariusz S. Jurgielewicz/Shutterstock; Globe © Anton Balazh/Shutterstock
Page 7: © Willyam Bradberry/Shutterstock
Page 8: Beach © Eugene Kalenkovich/Shutterstock; Globe © leonello calvetti/Shutterstock
Page 9: © Willyam Bradberry/Shutterstock
Page 10: Humpback whales © Catmando/Shutterstock; Globe © Anton Balazh/Shutterstock

Page 11: © Evocation Images/Shutterstock
Page 12: Antarctica © hecke61/Shutterstock; Globe © leonello calvetti/Shutterstock
Page 13: © Footage.Pro/Shutterstock
Page 14: North Pole © Evgeny Kovalev spb/Shutterstock; Globe © leonello calvetti/Shutterstock
Page 15: © Kotomiti Okuma/Shutterstock
Page 16: Puzzle pieces © Lim ChewHow/Shutterstock; Fish © Vilainecrevette/Shutterstock
Page 17: © simonalvinge/Shutterstock
Page 18: © Alexander Gordeyev /Shutterstock
Page 19: © riekephotos/Shutterstock
Page 20: © Nightman1965/Shutterstock
Page 21: © Dennis Sabo/Shutterstock
Page 22: © PRILL/Shutterstock

Page 23: Photo courtesy of Sylvia Earle
Page 24: © Sean Pavone/Shutterstock
Page 25: © Vlue/Shutterstock
Pages 26-27: © Fabien Monteil/Shutterstock
Page 28: © Isabelle Kuehn/Shutterstock
Page 29: © Fotosenmeer/Shutterstock

The author wishes to thank her wonderful grandchildren Elizabeth, Grace, Tommy and William Oltmans for being her inspiration.

BBM would like to thank the American Library Association for their dedication to education and children's literacy. Please visit their website for more information about the ways libraries and librarians make the world a better place: www.ala.org. For information on programs for young adults visit www.ala.org/yalsa.

For Dr. Sylvia Earle in recognition of her contributions to the conservation of ocean life

Remember that it is never a good idea to touch plants and creatures in their natural habitats. To help protect the oceans, you should never touch living coral or any other undersea creatures you encounter when swimming.

The ocean is full of LIFE!

Thousands of species of fish, big and small, live in the ocean. The largest animal, the blue whale, is as big as an airplane. Some of the smallest living things in the ocean are called plankton. They are so small that they can only be seen with a microscope. In between are animals of all sizes such as dolphins, sea otters and corals.

Many types of seaweeds, algae and plants live in the ocean. They provide food and homes for marine animals. They also provide an amazing amount of oxygen – in the water for marine animals but also in the air for us on land!

Ocean Fun Fact

Seaweeds aren't really weeds; they are important food sources for underwater creatures as well as humans, and many experts prefer to call them "sea vegetables."

5

Did you know that most of our planet is covered by one large, interconnected ocean? The largest, deepest ocean basin with the greatest variety of marine life living in it is the Pacific Ocean. It covers one-third of our planet.

Pacific Ocean

Ocean Fun Fact

The Pacific Ocean's name has an original meaning of "peaceful sea."

The Atlantic Ocean is our second largest ocean basin. Lying deep under the waters of the Atlantic is the longest mountain range in the world, called the Mid-Atlantic Ridge. It is almost as long as the planet.

Atlantic Ocean

Ocean Fun Fact

The underwater world is a mysterious place. People didn't explore the Mid-Atlantic Ridge until 1973. That was four years after Neil Armstrong and Buzz Aldrin walked on the moon!

The third largest ocean basin is the Indian Ocean. It is the warmest ocean in the world and is famous for strong winds and monsoons. Humpback whales live in the Indian Ocean as well as other places.

Indian
Ocean

Ocean Fun Fact

The Indian Ocean was known as "Ratnakara" in ancient literature. *Ratnakara* means "the maker of jewels."

The Antarctic Ocean is located around the South Pole. Also known as the Southern Ocean basin, this ocean is the home of emperor penguins and wandering albatrosses.

Ocean Fun Fact

Some geographers disagree on whether the Southern Ocean is its own ocean basin or just part of the Pacific, Atlantic and Indian Ocean basins.

Antarctic Ocean

Antarctic Ocean

The final ocean basin is the Arctic at the North Pole. The icy coasts and ice fields of the Arctic Ocean basin are where polar bears live.

Arctic
Ocean

North Pole

Ocean Fun Fact

"Arctic" comes from a Greek word meaning "near the bear."

All living creatures in the ocean depend on each other to live. They all fit together like puzzle pieces and create an ecosystem, or a community. Each part of the community works together to make life healthy for everyone.

Without the ocean, the world would be a completely different place. Have you seen pictures of what it is like on the surface of Mars or the Moon? Can you imagine what it would be like to have no oceans or rivers?

There are many problems facing our oceans: pollution, climate change and overfishing are just a few of them. The good news is that there are lots of people working all the time to try to make things better.

Ocean Fun Fact

Overfishing means that too many of a certain kind of fish have been caught in an area. If one kind of fish doesn't exist there anymore, it will affect all the other animal and plant life that live in that area and change the ecosystem.

Who helps protect the Ocean?

There are many men and women all over the world working in many different careers who are helping to clean up the ocean and make it safe. The truth is that almost anyone can help.

There are scientists who study the ocean to learn more about it, so that we know how to take better care of it and understand how the ocean affects the world and all the living things in it. The study of the ocean is called oceanography, and people who study it are called oceanographers.

Another career that provides opportunities to help ocean life is marine biology. A marine biologist studies the creatures – plants and animals – that live in the ocean or other bodies of water.

One famous marine biologist is Dr. Sylvia Earle. She discovered that she loved nature when she was a little girl in New Jersey. She would explore the woods near her home and study the plants and animals she saw there. When she was older, her family moved to Florida, and she grew to love the ocean too. Later in life, she turned her passion for nature and the ocean into a career.

She also started a program called Mission Blue, which establishes marine protected areas around the globe. These "Hope Spots" give the creatures that live in them a safe home. Endangered underwater species can begin to rebuild their numbers. Restoring endangered animals restores balance to the whole ecosystem.

"People ask, why should I care about the ocean? Because the ocean is the cornerstone of Earth's life support system, it shapes climate and weather. It holds most of life on Earth. Ninety-seven percent of Earth's water is there. It's the blue heart of the planet — we should take care of our heart. It's what makes life possible for us. We still have a really good chance to make things better than they are. They won't get better unless we take the action and inspire others to do the same thing. No one is without power. Everybody has the capacity to do something."

—Sylvia Earle

What can you do to help?

First, you can choose not to use plastic straws, single-use disposable bottles and plastic bags that are used for only a short time and then thrown away to create more pollution. Instead, use your own cloth bags, and reusable bottles and straws.

Next, tell other people about how important the ocean is and what they can do to help protect it. Make posters for your school. When you have to write a report, write about ocean life. Let everyone know that the ocean and the life within it are important to you. You can inspire others to start thinking about ways they can help.

Join in when there is a community

Large amounts of trash wash up on beaches every day. If everybody helps out, all of our beaches can be beautiful every day.

Ocean Fun Fact

A lot of the trash in our oceans comes from the rivers that empty into the oceans. So, even if you live far away from the beach, you can help keep the oceans cleaner by helping to pick up trash around the rivers and streams in your community.

Finally, never stop learning! The more you know about our ocean and the life within it, the more you might see new ways you can help make a difference.

Ocean Fun Fact

Baby sea turtles use moonlight to find their way to the water at night. Artificial lighting can confuse them and causes them to head inland instead, which is dangerous. So when you stay near a beach, try to use only natural light to help protect the sea turtles!

Remember that we can all help to make the world a cleaner, safer, better place by just doing our best every day. Change may be slow, but anything is possible if we all work together.

Here are some organizations that work to protect the ocean and the many living things that depend on it:

Jean-Michel Cousteau's Ocean Futures Society
www.oceanfutures.org

Mission Blue: The Sylvia Earle Alliance
mission-blue.org

NOAA Office of National Marine Sanctuaries
www.sanctuaries.noaa.gov

National Marine Sanctuary Foundation
www.nmsfocean.org

World Wildlife Fund
www.worldwildlife.org

Conservation International
www.conservation.org

Washed Ashore
www.washedashore.org

The Ocean Project
www.TheOceanProject.org

PERSEUS Project
www.perseus-net.eu

Reef Check
www.reefcheck.org

Woods Hole Oceanographic Institution
www.whoi.edu

Whale and Dolphin Conservation Society
www.whales.org

U.S. Fish & Wildlife Services
www.fws.gov

Endangered Species International
www.endangeredspecies international.org

PANACEA Project
www.panaceaproject.net

The Oceania Project
www.oceania.org.au

The Gray Whale Foundation
www.graywhalefoundation.org

Australian Institute of Marine Science
www.aims.gov.au

Gray Whales Count
www.graywhalescount.org

Alaska SeaLife Center
www.alaskasealife.org

SeaDoc Society
www.seadocsociety.org

IUCN Red List of Threatened Species™
www.iucnredlist.org

Marine Conservation Institute
www.marine-conservation.org

Fondation Prince Albert II de Monaco
www.institut-ocean.org

Marine Stewardship Council
www.msc.org

The Nature Conservancy
www.nature.org

Ocean Conservancy
www.oceanconservancy.org

One More Generation
www.onemoregeneration.org

International Ocean Institute
www.ioinst.org
www.ioikids.net

The Ocean Cleanup Foundation
www.theoceancleanup.com

National Marine Mammal Foundation
www.nmmf.org

UCSB-Coal Oil Point Reserve
coaloilpoint.ucnrs.org

Oceanic Preservation Society
www.opsociety.org

Fauna & Flora International
www.fauna-flora.org

Thank You Ocean
www.thankyouocean.org

ARKive.org
www.ARKive.org

The Pew Charitable Trusts
www.PewTrusts.org

Save The Whales
www.savethewhales.org

These zoos and aquariums are working to protect the ocean and it's inhabitants. For more information, visit their websites or, better yet, visit their locations:

California Academy of Sciences
www.calacademy.org

National Aquarium
www.aqua.org

The Association of Zoos and Aquariums
www.aza.org

Aquarium of the Pacific
www.aquariumofpacific.org

Tennessee Aquarium
www.tnaqua.org

ABQ BioPark
www.abqbiopark.com

Mote Marine Laboratory and Aquarium
www.mote.org

Point Defiance Zoo & Aquarium
www.pdza.org

Birch Aquarium at Scripps Institution of Oceanography
www.aquarium.ucsd.edu

Aquarium of the Bay
www.aquariumofthebay.org

Monterey Bay Aquarium
www.montereybayaquarium.org

Cabrillo Marine Aquarium
www.cabrillomarineaquarium.org

The Maritime Aquarium at Norwalk
www.maritimeaquarium.org

Georgia Aquarium
www.georgiaaquarium.org

The Florida Aquarium
www.flaquarium.org